PORTFOLIO 11

METROPOLITAN SEMINARS IN ART

Portfolio 11 · *The Artist*

by John Canaday

CHIEF OF THE DIVISION OF EDUCATION
THE PHILADELPHIA MUSEUM OF ART

THE METROPOLITAN MUSEUM OF ART

THE ARTIST

The Artist as a Social Critic

BY POPULAR conception the artist is an individual at odds with the conventional world (the artist as a rebel) or free from its conventions (the artist as a bohemian) or a dweller in some Cloud-Cuckoo-Land where he is less than half conscious of the world and its practical demands. He is ordinarily thought of as a man unconcerned with the social problems of his time.

In general the history of painting bears out this last assumption. The most enduring paintings are not likely to be comments on the passing scene, simply because that is what it is —passing. Art is concerned with permanent values, not transient ones. Its ultimate statement is general, not specific, even when it is couched in specific terms. In this portfolio, however, we will see some paintings stemming directly from affairs of the moment where the artist appears in his least familiar guise, as a social critic or reporter.

What we call "social consciousness," the awareness of the individual that he has a personal responsibility for the general good, is a relatively new idea. And it is not on the whole one that has inspired very much first-rate painting, if by first-rate one means painting that appeals universally instead of depending on topical subject matter for its meaning. How much a picture can lose when its topical associations are no longer current is shown in Daumier's lithograph *Rue Transnonain, April 15, 1834* (*Figure 1*), which appeared in Paris that same month. Neither the name of the street nor the date means anything to most people. Quizzed, perhaps the best they might do would be to guess that April might be the month the chestnut trees come into bloom along the Champs Élysées, something hard to connect with the scene in the picture, the aftermath of some appalling violence.

A man and woman lie dead on the floor of a bedroom. There has been a struggle; furniture is overturned, blood is spattered here and there and trickles from the bodies. Under the man lies the body of a child; the head of another corpse, an older man, whom we take to be the grandfather, shows at the right. It is a sobering picture, but anybody who looks at it, unless he knows the history of nineteenth-century France in some detail, is going to misinterpret it. It suggests to most people a sordid story of murder.

But on its appearance in 1834 with no other explanation than its title, the picture's association was entirely different. Workmen in Paris had been rioting in sympathetic demonstrations connected with a general strike called at Lyons. Troops patrolled the streets to keep order. In this state of near civil war they were fired upon from the windows of number 12, Rue Transnonain. In retaliation the soldiers killed every person in the building. Thus to Parisians, still shocked by this crime, the picture, when it appeared a few days after the event, was not the record of a sordid anecdote but a monumental accusation. And understood in this light the picture changes character for us; the very room in which the bodies lie seems to grow more quiet, the bodies themselves acquire the stature of martyrs or significant victims, whereas before they were merely the detritus of human frailty.

None of this means that *Rue Transnonain* is less of a work of art than it set out to be. Daumier was serving a special circumstance. Upon its appearance the picture must have carried a staggering impact and still carries one when we become acquainted with the situation that produced it. But the circumstance remains special, which is why the picture is used here as an example of the limitations that affect the artist whose comment is topical.

Social Cruelty

To show that a painting may rise above topical limitations even when it begins with a topical subject we can compare *Rue Transnonain* with Goya's similar subject, *The Executions of the Third of May* (Plate 121).

The executions Goya depicts took place in 1808, the year of the Napoleonic conquest of Spain. The king and the army had hardly resisted the French invasion, which was accomplished with a maximum of pointless brutality, if we are to trust Goya's records of it, and occupation was regarded with a minimum of concern by an incomparably contemptible Spanish ruling class.

But then, in Madrid, the people learned that the son of the king was to be carried away to France. Whether he stayed or went made no practical difference, but to the people he was a symbol. Thus the Madrileños, protecting the monarchy whose members were doing their best to ingratiate themselves with Napoleon, attacked the invaders in the streets. This was the Second of May, the date that marked the beginning of Napoleon's expulsion.

The uprising of the Second of May was followed on the next day by frightful reprisals. Civilians were executed in group lots without much regard for their guilt or innocence as participants in the fighting. Possession of a penknife was called carrying arms, and, according to one account, even the ownership of a pair of scissors was enough to establish guilt and bring a sentence of death.

Goya shows one of the civilian executions in *The Executions of the Third of May*, in which a group of Madrileños faces the firing squad. At their feet sprawl human carcasses, while beyond them the next lot of victims stands in line. The scene takes place against a barren rise of ground; in the distance the outlying buildings of the city are spectral.

Now, while all these elements are historically identifiable, the picture goes beyond the immediate circumstance to make a statement applicable at any time in history. For a Spaniard the historical context no doubt endows the painting with particular excitement. Yet this context also imposes a limitation. If we know nothing about the Second of May as a historical event, the picture's dramatic power is at least as great. It is even more inclusive, for the picture's effectiveness is widened when the connotations are no longer tied to a single event or a single country.

The picture centers around a young man who flings up his arms and thrusts his body forward (*Figure 2*) as if to demonstrate his complete vulnerability as an individual and yet to defy the soldiers with the jibe that this execution will not affect the cause for which he stands. He is the spirit of a revolt that will continue against all odds because it is beyond personal defeat or annihilation. At his shoulder a half-brutish companion senses this conviction. Half comprehending, he too thrusts himself forward to receive the bullets. The other figures and those in line stare or hide their faces in various reactions of horror, despair, or resignation.

In contrast to the excitement, variety, and humanity of the figures of the victims, the executioners are ranged in identical poses suggesting automatons, their faces hidden so that they are further de-individualized. Thus they

Print Department, Boston Public Library

Figure 1

become figures of blind force, ultimately incapable of victory because they are not endowed with passion and perception.

If Goya had chosen to make us aware of the psychological state of each soldier as an individual, the point of the picture would be lost. If the soldiers were represented as a group of unmitigated villains we would sense that the artist was stacking the cards. Soldiers selected as members of a firing squad are human beings also; they also react in a variety of ways to the job at hand. But Goya wants no interplay of human emotions here. He is painting unquenchable passion for freedom in the face of any force attempting to stem it, and he does it by ranging human beings against symbols of insensate power.

Daumier's *Rue Transnonain* and Goya's *The Executions of the Third of May* were done within about twenty years of one another. As we come forward in history from the early nineteenth century, examples of "socially conscious" painting occur more and more frequently. As we go back we find examples in the eighteenth century, which we will see shortly in this portfolio, but before that time they appear only occasionally and even then eccentrically. We will compare an extraordinary example from the end of the fifteenth century with a corresponding one painted more than four hundred years later.

The first is Botticelli's *Calumny* (Plate 122), painted just before 1500 in renaissance Italy. The second is a contemporary American picture, Ben Shahn's *Passion of Sacco and Vanzetti* (Plate 123), one of a series painted only a few decades ago, in 1932. On the surface the two pictures appear to have no similarities at all, yet they have unexpected parallels when they are examined more deeply.

Botticelli's *Calumny* is a curious picture and not altogether a pleasing one. The extreme complications of line are an exaggeration of Botticelli's earlier style, which we have already seen at its happiest in *La Primavera* (Plate 58, Portfolio 5).

In the center of the composition we see an innocent victim dragged by the hair to judgment by Calumny, who carries a torch, a false symbol of her love of truth. Two other female figures flank her and twine roses in her hair. These are Calumny's attendants, Fraud and Deception. The standing male figure in this central group, dressed in rags, is Envy, who makes his false accusations to the Judge.

Although the Judge wears a crown and carries a scepter he also has ass's ears. Ignorance whispers into one ear, Suspicion into the other, and he listens.

All these figures are snarled and knotted into groups with lines of such complication that the effect they create is finally—and appropriately—grotesque and disagreeable. They occupy the major portion of the picture space, filling it with masses of twisting draperies, writhing hair, and oddly jointed limbs that weave in and out of one another like nests of serpents. If we compare the heads and arms of the three female figures, Calumny, Fraud, and Deception (*Figure 3*), with those of the Three Graces (*Figure 4*) from *La Primavera* we can see how tortured confusion replaces the rhythmic linear harmony of the earlier picture. But the artist uses this disturbing line only where it is appropriate.

In one figure he gives us again a line of great simplicity and purity. This is the figure of Truth, who stands naked at the extreme left, ignored and all but crowded out of the scene, connected with the other figures only by the glance of one who turns and regards her with prophetic questioning. She is Remorse, an ancient crone in black rags.

The allegory is taken directly from the description by Lucian of a vanished painting by the ancient Greek artist Apelles. But it is improbable that Botticelli painted *Calumny* simply as an exercise in the reconstruction of a lost masterpiece. Classical allegory was frequently Botticelli's vehicle of expression (as we

Photo by Anderson

Figure 2

have already mentioned in Portfolio 5), and, for that matter, it was the most popular one of the time for the propounding of moral judgments. In his *Calumny* Botticelli may have been concealing a specific accusation against society in the guise of a general allegory.

One theory is that *Calumny* allegorizes the political attacks on the Medici family, Botticelli's great patrons, that resulted in their exile from Florence after they had ruled it for several generations. The crime the artist pictures takes place within a loggia of purest classical-renaissance design embellished with works of art, a setting that would symbolize Florence at the apogee of its cultivation under Medici patronage, now defiled by the monstrous event being enacted there. The deep serenity of the sea and sky opening out beyond the noble arcade is a final contrast to the hysterical violence of the false trial.

The *Calumny* has often been interpreted as a concealed protest against the trial, conviction, and execution of the priest Savonarola. Today Savonarola would be called a revivalist. His apocalyptic sermons against the vanities of life, the corruption of power, and the moral decay of Italy in general made him for a while the most influential man in the city-state of Florence. He was a scholar and a man of God, but he was also a zealot and a fanatic. His power waned through the sheer exhaustion of his followers, who were unable to sustain his pitch of intensity. Savonarola, a menace to the temporal power of the Church as well as to the State, was eventually tried for heresy on charges that may or may not have been trumped-up. He was convicted after confessions made following an ordeal that may or may not have included physical torture. He was executed by hanging and then burned in the public square of Florence, where not long before he had achieved his most spectacular triumphs. His pyre was built on the same spot where he had held his famous "bonfires of vanities," burning great mounds of such irreligious objects as false hair, cosmetics, rich costumes, and works of art not dedicated to the highest moral principles, all delivered up to the fire by temporarily repentant Florentines.

Although Botticelli is known to have come under Savonarola's influence, it is not likely that *Calumny* is a specific reference to the martyred priest's trial, conviction, and execution, since most scholars believe the picture was painted before Savonarola was executed in 1498. The intensity of the painting, however, suggests an anguished protest against the spirit of the witch-hunt, the punishment of innocent people who are sacrificed to public hysteria. Therein lies its parallel to the twentieth-century painting we are comparing with it, a picture speaking of the trial, conviction, and execution of two men, Nicola Sacco and Bartolomeo Vanzetti.

As in the case of Savonarola, the guilt or innocence of Sacco and Vanzetti was the subject of vehement controversy. The painter believed that they were the victims of a miscarriage of justice. We are not balancing the scales here but are examining the protest made in pictorial form by an artist in the light of his own belief, in order to compare it with a similar subject approached in a different way.

Botticelli's painting accuses the Florentine government of ignorance, suspicion, envy, calumny, fraud, and deception, depicts it as unworthy of the crown and scepter of authority, proclaims the victim's innocence, and prophesies the city's remorse, all this in allegorical concealment; the modern painting makes parallel accusations with no effort whatsoever at disguising the message. In *The Passion of Sacco and Vanzetti* all subtleties and indirections are abandoned for an uncompromising indictment. Nicola Sacco was a fish peddler and philosophical anarchist; Bartolomeo Vanzetti a shoe factory employee and radical agitator. In 1920 they were accused of killing two men in a payroll holdup at South Braintree, Massachusetts, and found guilty. But for six years liberals everywhere campaigned for their release on grounds that prejudice had convicted the men; essentially, that they were being convicted as a philosophical anarchist and a radical agitator rather than as killers in a holdup.

A series of sensational appeals culminated in the appointment of a committee of three headed by President Lowell of Harvard and including the then president of the Massachusetts Institute of Technology and a former judge. It was the opinion of this committee that the verdict of guilty should be sustained, and sentence of death on Sacco and Vanzetti was carried out in the prison at Charlestown, Massachusetts, on August 22, 1927. But a large body of considered opinion continued to believe the two men innocent.

Calumny and *The Passion of Sacco and Vanzetti* have a very close similarity of pictorial procedure beneath their primary difference of style. In *The Passion of Sacco and Vanzetti* the victims are not shown dragged naked to false judgment but are revealed in their coffins after execution. It does not take a great stretch of the imagination to associate the half-caricatured figure in academic cap and gown with Botticelli's figure of Calumny. He is flanked

Photo by Anderson

Figure 3

Photo by Anderson

Figure 4

by two top-hatted figures holding lilies in their hands. They are certainly parallels to Fraud and Deception, the female figures who twine roses in Calumny's hair. Their roses and the lilies borne by the top-hatted figures are the same false symbols of purity.

The parallel continues. Botticelli's unworthily crowned and sceptered false Judge is repeated in Shahn's painting by a framed portrait of the sentencing judge in the Sacco-Vanzetti case, his hand raised in a gesture suggesting at once the oath of truth or a gesture of benediction, either one of which would be desperately ironical. This portrait hangs in the hall of a neoclassical court building corresponding to Botticelli's allegorical renaissance palace. The only element without correspondence is the group of Remorse and Truth—if, indeed, the lamp in the upper left corner of the modern picture is not intended to be some such reference.

The four pictures we have seen so far have taken their subjects from specific instances of social cruelty or injustice. In varying degree they accepted or overcame the limitation that can keep this kind of picture from being a complete expression in its own right—the limitation, that is, of the observer's being dependent on knowledge of the specific event for full understanding of the picture's meaning. Even without this knowledge, even if we are left to find for ourselves their general sense, they are works of art of interpretative power or, at least, of curious fascination.

Social Ideas

As a contrast, we may compare these pictures with John Trumbull's *The Declaration of Independence* (Plate 124)—in doing so we take the risk of being unfair to this worthy and much loved painting by putting it into brilliant company that makes it look more pedestrian than it is. Trumbull shows assembled in a room of admirable colonial style a group of dignified gentlemen conducting themselves with extraordinary decorum. The features of each participant are as true to life as Trumbull could make them, but in spite of the general solemnity and the air of consequence they have assumed, there is not much indication that the gentlemen are present at a climactic moment in the history of the modern world. They could easily be doing nothing more important than granting a charter to some minor institution or signing one of those bothersome expressions of esteem that corporations have a habit of preparing for retiring directors. The social idealism, the political conflict, the prescience of war and sacrifice, in short, all the significant historical and emotional elements of a great moment in the course of human events are not hinted at. Reducing our criticism to irreverent terms, the shortcoming in Trumbull's depiction of the signing of the Declaration of Independence on the first Fourth of July is that he has omitted fireworks. What do these impassive effigies have to do with the glory and the spiritual magnificence of the birth of a great nation?

Does *The Declaration of Independence* fall short because it lacks the vehemence of *The Executions of the Third of May*, the intensity of *Calumny*, or the high moral purpose of *The Passion of Sacco and Vanzetti*? Perhaps it does—as an independent picture out of its context. But it is a richer picture when it is considered as a reflection of the spirit of the time when it was conceived. The picture we reproduce here is one of four studies painted by Trumbull shortly after the end of the Revolution that he was later commissioned to repeat for the rotunda of the Capitol building in Washington (the other three being *The Surrender of Cornwallis at Yorktown*, *The Surrender of Burgoyne at Saratoga*, and *Washington Resigning His Commission*). The new nation, anxious to take its place with the established countries of the world, was more interested in proclaiming its dignity and solidity than its fire and imagination. The new Capitol was no country-bumpkin of a building but a monument in the tradition of the great structures of ancient Rome, as revived and modified in the nations of the modern world. To maintain a harmony with this architectural setting it was necessary to select paintings that were imagined in the same faintly pompous spirit—a requirement that, it must be admitted, was perfectly compatible with Trumbull's own ideas. Ideally the four panels chosen to adorn the Capitol should have been conceived with a dignity and nobility that translated into visual terms Thomas Jefferson's masterpiece, the Declaration itself. But there was no artist in America with stature as a painter equal to Jefferson's as a statesman, and there was no European painter who could have thought and painted in terms of Jefferson's political idealism. As a result we have Trumbull's *Declaration of Independence*, a little dull and unimaginative if forced to compete with other pictures as a complete and expressive statement in itself, yet having an appropriateness in the setting of its own time and its own place that dignifies and enriches it.

A few decades later the Frenchman Eugène Delacroix painted his emotionalized *Liberty Leading the People* (Plate 125), a fine, swirling, highly charged expression of the social ferment that led to revolutionary disorders in France in 1830. Both *The Declaration of Independence*

The Louvre Museum, Paris, photo by Archives Photographiques

Figure 5

Figure 6

and *Liberty Leading the People* are concerned with the same theme. If we try to imagine the Delacroix substituted for the Trumbull as an ornament for the national Capitol, however, it suddenly looks forced and high-flown, although no critic would seriously question its superiority over the American painting as the solution of a problem of expression.

What all this comes down to is that the essence of an event cannot be expressed simply by reproducing its circumstances. The painter with something to say about the history of his time may be wiser to forget factual appearances and depend on other ways of putting across his ideas. This is what Delacroix was doing when he painted *Liberty Leading the People*, and, less obviously, it is what Goya was doing in *The Executions of the Third of May*, which is an imagined, a created version of an actual event, not a reproduction of it.

Style and Social Statement

And of course a painter may want to comment on the contemporary scene without referring specifically to it in the image he creates. Jacques Louis David's *The Death of Socrates* (Plate 126) is an instance. Although the subject is drawn from the ancient world David's reference is to his own France. The old philosopher, about to drink his cup of hemlock poison, illustrates the ideal of self-sacrifice for a principle; likewise, the noble cause of the French Revolution required sacrifices by those who believed in it. *The Death of Socrates* is a work of almost icy elegance, immaculately drawn and painted. Its surface is as tight and smooth as enamel, and the edges of its forms are sharp, clear, and uncompromising. In spite of a certain staginess the arrangement is also severe, or at least it is very severe in comparison with the tradition against which it revolted. A typical example of this tradition, Boucher's *The Toilet of Venus* (Plate 127), will show us why *The Death of Socrates* was a radically "modern" picture and why its technique was part and parcel of a new social philosophy.

The Toilet of Venus was painted for an eighteenth-century French court society in which women determined much of the policy and for which they certainly dictated the taste. Whether applied to a bedroom, a sitting room, a court hall, or a chapel, fashionable décor consistently suggested the boudoir. Paintings were liberally incorporated into these decorative schemes as ornamental panels. Boucher, with pictures like *The Toilet of Venus*, was an immense success because he developed a manner completely in harmony with the feminine delicacy of the style.

His typical female figure is a young girl of chubby proportions with dewy lips, wide eyes, blond hair, and an air of perverse innocence suggesting more than anything else the pleasures of seduction. In *The Toilet of Venus* she happens to be posed as the goddess of love and beauty, but even when Boucher painted milkmaids they were girls of the same cut surrounded by the same opulent, fashionable swirls of taffetas, flowers, and ornamental paraphernalia. *The Toilet of Venus* suggests every feminine refinement of erotic pleasure; it is a perfumed, sweet-flavored painting, at once as fresh as the blossoms strewn about in it, as expensive as the jewels of the goddess, and as calculated as the wiles of a professional courtesan. It is a superb professional job created for a limited audience, an audience of specialized cultivation with the means to indulge itself in the acquisition of every accessory to this cultivation, from desirable partners to fine or fashionable works of art.

Indirectly a picture like *The Toilet of Venus* is a social comment even though the painter had no trace of such an idea in mind. In earlier portfolios of this series in our discussions of painting as an expression of its time we examined a painting by one of Boucher's contemporaries, Chardin. His still life of simple homely objects (Plate 20, Portfolio 2) was conceived in a spirit the reverse of Boucher's slick and superficial one. The two painters represent opposing factors in eighteenth-century culture: Chardin represents the new philosophical interest in the common man and the nobility of simple things; Boucher, the tag end of the renaissance period of luxury and power concentrated in inherited position. It was this conflict, we know, that at the end of the century tore France apart in the Revolution.

In the light of the burgeoning French Revolution David's *Death of Socrates* begins to make new sense. The revolutionary spirit was a denial of every quality of the *ancien régime* summarized in Boucher's *The Toilet of Venus*; it was a proclamation of new social standards. Masculine decision must dominate feminine sensitivity; self-sacrifice must replace self-indulgence. Moral force becomes the paramount virtue, opposing its parallel vice, the cultivation of sensuous pleasures. Opulence gives way to austerity, fashionable invention to philosophical order.

When *The Toilet of Venus* and *The Death of Socrates* are placed side by side, it should be apparent that *The Death of Socrates*, for all its elegance as seen in retrospect, proclaims these new ideals. Its revolutionary approach is more apparent if we know that as a student young

Figure 7

David was greatly influenced by Boucher and even did a competition picture, *The Combat of Minerva and Mars* (*Figure 5*), in a windy adaptation of Boucher's style. But as a fledgling painter in Rome he departed from this manner to develop the severe, highly disciplined one that helped make him one of the powerful figures in the Revolutionary government.

Instead of a seductive adolescent goddess in her boudoir David paints a philosopher surrounded by his loyal followers. But subject matter aside, the choice and delineation of forms in the two pictures contrast correspondingly. As an instance, some of the drapery passages in the David are of great beauty (*Figure 6*), but it is a beauty of discipline and order as opposed to the profligate gaiety of Boucher's taffetas (*Figure 7*). Compositionally the antithesis continues. The Boucher is designed in swirls and graceful curves; forms coquettishly play in and out of the picture depth. Objects are piled and strewn about with wanton abandon. But the David gives an immediate impression of absolute control. Each figure is placed uncompromisingly, posed almost rigidly, in a scheme where every detail is calculated to the last degree.

The Toilet of Venus is just as skillfully and even more subtly organized; the point is that its organization is directed to give an impression of lightness and spontaneity, whereas *The Death of Socrates* insists upon formal order as a virtue and calls our attention to the fact that every element in the picture is subject to its unyielding discipline.

Compared with the half-illustrative, half-symbolical approach of *The Passion of Sacco and Vanzetti*, the social statement of *The Death of Socrates* seems to be made in a roundabout way. But in the long run—and art is always a matter of the long run—*The Passion of Sacco and Vanzetti* will grow more and more enigmatic, while *The Death of Socrates* should continue to speak of high idealism, dedication, and sacrifice, whether or not any connection is made between it and the events that once surrounded it.

We referred a few paragraphs ago to the eighteenth-century philosophical conception of the innate nobility of simple things and the simple man. In the nineteenth century this idea

Museum of Fine Arts, Boston

Figure 8

Private collection, courtesy of the San Francisco Museum of Art

Figure 9

was given enough sentimental flavoring to make it palatable to a wide public in the art of Jean François Millet, whose *The Sower* (*Figure 8*) has come to be one of the best-known pictures in the world. The figure of a full-bodied peasant played against the light of a late afternoon sky is reduced to a near-silhouette. Details of dress and features are obscured in the interest of monumental breadth; this powerful mass fills the picture space and takes on an importance that the figure would not have if it were smaller in relation to the space or if objects in the immediate background were allowed to compete with it. If, for instance, the fields were shown stretching beyond the sower on every side, as of course they would in visual fact, leaving him isolated, surrounded by earth and sky, he could have become a symbol of man's smallness in the vastness of the world. As it is, the fields behind him suggest this vastness, but he dominates it, making us aware of the final importance of the man who tills and sows and reaps, without whom the structure of society could not exist. Also, working in rhythm with the cycle of nature, he is presumably closer to something of ultimate significance than the rest of us are. This idea is expressed in "Saison des Semailles—Le Soir" (translated "The Sower") by Victor Hugo, which echoes the painting:

C'est le moment crépusculaire.
J' admire, assis sous un portail,
Ce reste de jour dont s'éclaire
La dernière heure du travail.

Dans les terres, de nuit baignées,
Je contemple, ému, les haillons
D'un vieillard qui jette à poignées
La moisson future aux sillons.

Sa haute silhouette noire
Domine les profonds labours.
On sent à quel point il doit croire
A la fuite utile des jours.

Il marche dans la plaine immense,
Va, vient, lance la graine au loin,
Rouvre sa main, et recommence,
Et je médite, obscur témoin,

Pendant que, déployant ses voiles,
L'ombre, où se mêle une rumeur,
Semble élargir jusqu'aux étoiles
Le geste auguste du semeur.

It is twilight. From my doorstep I am gazing where the ray
Lights the latest hour of labour from the dying of the day.

Not unmoved, amid the furrows bathed in night a hind I see
Old and ragged, scattering broadcast seed of harvests yet to be.

How his tall black outline towers against the background of his toil!
What a trust is his in time, that yields the increase of the soil!

On the hedgeless plain he paces, comes and goes, and throws the seed;
Dips his hand and recommences; from my corner, I give heed

How the shadows, gently rustling as they draw their curtain lower,
Seem to widen round the stars the kingly gesture of the Sower.

Translation by Sir George Young

The romantic and ideal peasant as a kind of earth-symbol is all very well, but the lot of the nineteenth-century peasant was a little less

Figure 10

than ideal when he was thought of as a human being. At close range Nature's Nobleman had a distressing way of looking more like Society's Victim, a variation on Millet's theme that did not escape him even if he seldom dealt with it. In at least one picture, however, he showed the peasant as a creature brutalized by labor and poverty, the famous *Man with the Hoe* (*Figure 9*), which inspired another poet, Edwin Markham, to a comment different from Hugo's:

Bowed by the weight of centuries he leans
Upon his hoe and gazes on the ground,
The emptiness of ages in his face,
And on his back the burden of the world.
Who made him dead to rapture and despair,
A thing that grieves not and that never hopes,
Stolid and stunned, a brother to the ox?
Who loosened and let down this brutal jaw?
Whose was the hand that slanted back this brow?
Whose breath blew out the light within this brain?

Is this the Thing the Lord God made and gave
To have dominion over sea and land;
To trace the stars and search the heavens for power;
To feel the passion of Eternity?

The position of the French peasant some hundred years ago was neither as desperate as that of *The Man with the Hoe* nor as pleasant as that of the rest of Millet's simple men, but the position of the Mexican peon at the beginning of this century was without question subhuman. In *The Liberation of the Peon* (Plate 128), also called *The Death of the Peon*, Diego Rivera commemorates the social rescue of the Mexican peasant by the Agrarian Revolution.

Rivera, who was discussed in Portfolio 8 in connection with a revival of fresco painting in this century, was commissioned to paint a series of murals for the Ministry of Education (*Figure 10*) in Mexico City, an undertaking he started in 1923. He conceived them as a combination of historical fact, ancient legend, and

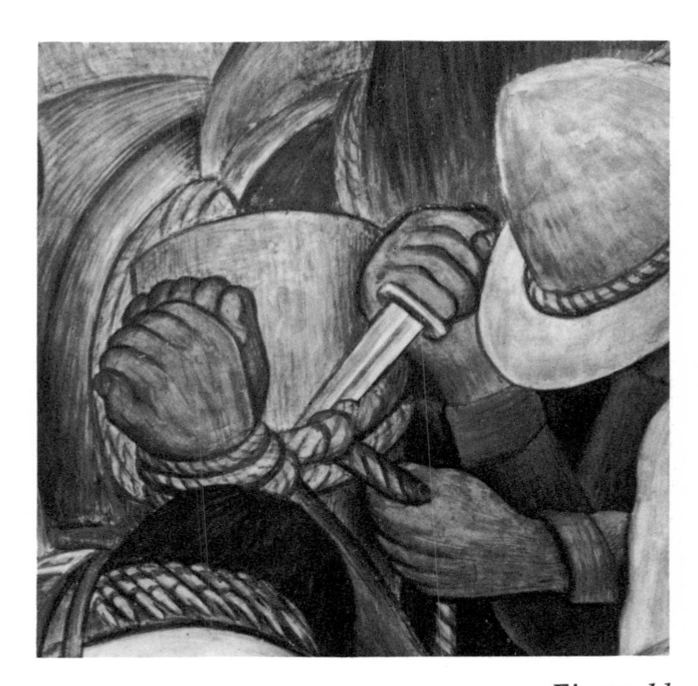

Figure 11

sociological and political propaganda—a combination just as original but more harmonious than it sounds. The standard approaches for such commissions for the ornamentation of public buildings had crystallized into two familiar, threadbare forms. The more familiar was the obvious series of stuffy storytelling scenes in which historical figures stand around in costume like so many dummies in waxworks' tableaux of famous events. The second approach might be called the routine-symbolical, in which groups of well-built male and female models are painted in decorative attitudes holding cornucopias, shields, torches, scrolls, parts of machines (very advanced), and so on for the amount of wall space to be covered, and labeled prosperity, law, justice, art, industry.

Rivera fell victim to neither of these bromides. His frescoes cover walls around open courts, and, read in sequence, they are a vivid propagandistic textbook where the illiterate may read the history of Mexico in terms of agrarian-revolutionist ideology. *The Liberation of the Peon* symbolizes the end of an era of persecution and exploitation of the common Mexican and the beginning of his

Ministry of Education, Mexico City

Figure 12

Figure 13

Photo by Anderson

Figure 14

liberation in the sense of political rights, landownership, and education.

In the background of *The Liberation of the Peon* a hacienda of the oppressive landowning class is in flames. The revolutionists who have overthrown this regime are grouped around the peon, whose body is striped with whip marks. One symbolically cuts a rope that binds his wrists (*Figure 11*), another supports him gently, a third covers his dead nakedness.

Rivera's frescoes are stunning decorations and, frequently, works of art of high caliber aside from and often in spite of the insistent propagandistic fervor that sometimes defeats itself. It does so in *The Millionaires* (*Figure 12*) where Rockefeller, Morgan, and Ford are shown in caricature so vicious that it overshoots the mark and gives us a newspaper cartoon rather than a work of art with expressive extensions beyond its immediate subject. *The Liberation of the Peon* has these extensions.

Compositionally *The Liberation of the Peon* is built along a sweeping line running diagonally through the picture along the limp body of the victim. This line is countered by the head and neck of the horse in upper center, which turns the line back and leads us again toward the right. On both sides the movement is stabilized by standing figures with strong vertical axes—the horse on the left, the man holding a horse on the right. Within this framework there are secondary rhythms of highly geometrized loops made by the ammunition belts, the ropes, saddles, hats, and the simplified, rounded forms of the figures. In places this decorative geometry is strong enough to distract our attention from the whole, as it should not have been allowed to do. The pattern on the chest of the horse to the left, for instance, is too conspicuous for so incidental a detail; the crisscrossed loops of ammunition around the neck and chest of the standing figure at the right, the knot in the shirt, the design of the ropes (*Figure 13*) are also attractive enough to exist for themselves rather than as adjuncts to the whole. But in singling these out we are finding small flaws in a successful arrangement.

In beginning the murals Rivera experimented with using the juice of a Mexican cactus plant as his medium, an idea with special attractions for this particular commission, but it was not successful. He employed instead the pure fresco technique of fourteenth-century Italian painters. He also drew heavily upon their pictorial tradition. The relationship of *The Liberation of the Peon* to Pietàs and Descents from the Cross is apparent. The forms and the composition suggest Giotto's *Lamentation over the Body of Christ* (*Figure 14*) from the fresco series in the Arena Chapel in Padua painted in 1305. But it is one thing to depend parasitically upon a great tradition like that of fourteenth-century Italy and another to use it as a point of departure, as Rivera did. *The Liberation of the Peon* stands as a work of art in its own right whatever its borrowings from renaissance Italy or its adaptations of the forms of ancient Mexican art.

Hogarth's London

In 1732 the English painter William Hogarth published *A Harlot's Progress*, a set of six engravings recounting the story of an innocent country girl from her seduction upon arriving in the city through a career including prosperity, poverty, prison, disease, and death. Partly fiction with overtones of soap opera and partly social comment, the series was a financial success. Although Hogarth secretly regarded them as hack work, he published two more sets, *A Rake's Progress* and *Marriage à la Mode*, the latter detailing the misfortunes of a young couple in a loveless marriage arranged by selfish and ambitious parents.

These pictorial tracts have become classics in the history of art and cornerstones in the history of art as social comment. They are an amalgam of rather fuzzy moral preachments, lively satire, and explicit records of the contemporary scene, lifted to significance by the sudden appearance here and there of occasional scenes depicting some social cruelty. We will follow *A Rake's Progress* in some detail.

Sir John Soane's Museum, London

Figure 15

The first scene, *The Young Heir Takes Possession of the Miser's Effects* (*Figure 15*), is worth examining closely as an example of Hogarth's narrative method. We are told what is going on by pictorial signposts like letters, open diaries, and other written matter that we must actually read to understand the action. This method is an extremely unpainterly way of going about the job, as Hogarth very well knew, but he was working for popular response from a not very art-minded public, and he found this formula to be a successful one.

The signposts in *The Young Heir* show us a very young man, Tom Rakewell, called home from Oxford by the death of his father. There are a dozen indications that the father was a miser who managed to save a considerable fortune. There are just as many that Tom is getting ready to spend it. A strongbox full of silver has been broken open; beside it are heaps of securities—mortgages, bonds, and

Sir John Soane's Museum, London

Figure 16

Sir John Soane's Museum, London

Figure 17

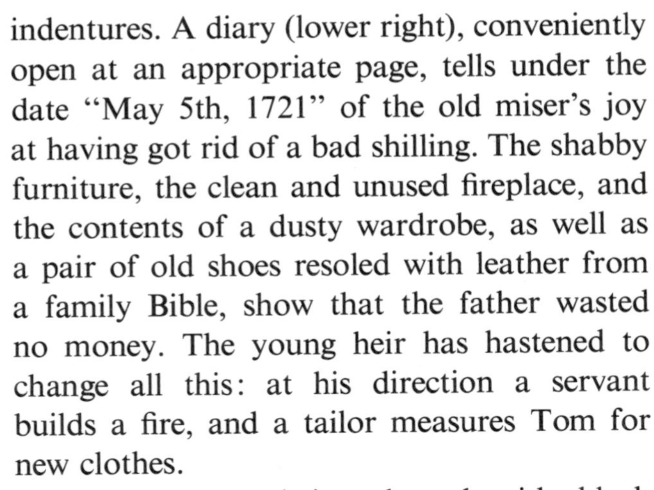

indentures. A diary (lower right), conveniently open at an appropriate page, tells under the date "May 5th, 1721" of the old miser's joy at having got rid of a bad shilling. The shabby furniture, the clean and unused fireplace, and the contents of a dusty wardrobe, as well as a pair of old shoes resoled with leather from a family Bible, show that the father wasted no money. The young heir has hastened to change all this: at his direction a servant builds a fire, and a tailor measures Tom for new clothes.

The walls are being draped with black mourning cloth, disturbing a rotten molding that drops a fall of gold coins. Near the window the miser's escutcheon shows three vises clamped tight, with the motto "Beware!" The jack and spit, symbols of hospitality, have been carefully kept locked up in a cubbyhole (upper right).

Tom is arguing with an irate mother who holds an apronful of his letters to her pregnant daughter, Sarah Young. Sarah, a good girl with whom Tom has had his way, weeps, holding his ring in one hand. Tom will pay her off with the sack of gold behind him, from which his lawyer filches a coin, a prophecy of the assaults he will make on the young rake's fortune on a still larger scale after they get to London.

In the second scene, *The Levée* (*Figure 16*), Tom is holding his gathering in the French (and to Hogarth, contemptible) manner. He is cultivating all the fashionable graces; hence his entourage, with identifiable portraits, includes a dancing master, a French fencing master who lunges with the shortsword, an English instructor in quarterstaff who looks on disapprovingly, a landscape architect, a professor of music at a harpsicord, a jockey with a trophy in the form of a silver bowl, presumably won by one of Tom's horses, and in the background tailors, perukemakers, hatmakers, and a poet who hopes for Tom's patronage. Portraits of fighting cocks on the wall show that the young blade is also interested in that sport.

Skipping the third scene for the moment, we find in the fourth scene, *The Arrest* (*Figure 17*), that our rake has made the grade socially and is on his way to be received at court. Or at least we learn it if we identify the palace of Saint James in the background and if we recognize, as Hogarth's contemporaries would, two figures to be Welshmen wearing enormous leeks, a symbol that fixes the day as the first of March, a day sacred to the titular saint of Wales and one observed by a reception at court. (If this seems far-fetched, think how easily today we would identify a date as

Sir John Soane's Museum, London

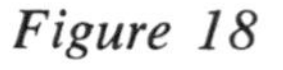

Figure 18

Sir John Soane's Museum, London

Figure 19

March 17 if a picture included an Irishman appropriately displaying a shamrock emblem and, perhaps, lining up for a parade.) It is easier for us to identify a bailiff who stops Tom's sedan chair and threatens him with arrest for debt. Bankrupt, Tom is saved by Sarah Young, now by her costume a milliner, who reappears on the scene, plausibly enough, to observe the dress of the people arriving at the reception. She pays the bailiff from her own purse.

This is Tom's chance for repentance and redemption, but in the next scene, *The Marriage* (*Figure 18*), we find him marrying a hideous old woman, obviously rich, who has accepted his proposal with such alacrity that her maid is still arranging her wedding gown at the ceremony. Tom is hardly able to hide his repugnance for his bride. Sarah, holding Tom's baby, stands in the background while her mother tries to battle her way into the chapel.

The story goes on with Tom's losing his new wife's fortune in a gaming house (*Figure 19*), follows him to debtor's prison (*Figure 20*) where Sarah Young, unable to help him further, falls in a faint while his hag of a wife berates him, and shows him in the last scene, *The Madhouse* (*Figure 21*), as he ends up in Bedlam, London's insane asylum, a maniac among maniacs, not even recognizing the faithful Sarah, who still stands by.

As a narrative *A Rake's Progress* is lively enough even if its situations have become trite after two centuries; as a moral lesson it is ambiguous because while vice is punished, virtue is not rewarded. As social comment it is largely satirical, but in the last two scenes, the debtor's prison and especially the one in Bedlam, it rises above itself.

In debtor's prison Tom has tried to write a play to recoup his fortunes. A rejection note lies beside him on the table. Behind him the turnkey presses for his prison fees, and an errand boy refuses to leave a mug of beer Tom has ordered but cannot pay for. The other inmates are so picturesque as to confuse the issue somewhat. The man who helps support Sarah is identified by a scroll as one "J. L. now a prisoner in the Fleet," giving us the name of the prison, who has been working on "a new scheme for paying the debts of the nation." And in the background another prisoner operates some chemical apparatus, possibly tied up with alchemy, while on the canopy of the bed (upper right) a pair of wings designed to be worn by a human being are a third symbol of visionary foolishness. In spite of these distractions, our attention is called to the squalor and hopelessness of Fleet Prison.

Sir John Soane's Museum, London

Figure 20

Sir John Soane's Museum, London

Figure 21

The scene in Bedlam (a corruption of Bethlehem) Hospital is more appalling. The inmates are a roster of standard insanities, the religious maniac, the naked man with delusions of grandeur, the hopeless depressive seated on the stairs, and various gibbering manic types. The two women in the background are visitors. Bedlam was open as a kind of side show for the public and according to contemporary records was a notorious meeting place for sexual intriguers.

To what extent was Hogarth actually protesting against the cruelty of social institutions in these pictures of Fleet Prison and Bedlam? Although he reveals them in all their foulness, he does not do much more than record the actual state of things. But the state of things was so bad that any truthful record had to constitute a protest.

Although another artist might have treated these subjects humorously or with the morbid, callous curiosity of the two women visitors to Bedlam, it must have been quite possible for Hogarth's contemporaries to miss the point of any implied criticism of the institutions, for the pictures did not reveal any conditions not well known to everybody. If *A Rake's Progress* is a moral lesson and Fleet Prison and Bedlam, for all their horrors, are only the hells to which our sinner is legitimately damned, then Hogarth's social protest is confused with his moral warning that his rake is getting no worse than he deserved. But since Hogarth once said that he would rather have "checked the progress of cruelty than been the author of Raphael's cartoons" we may take it that he had some such protest in mind.

Hogarth's engravings for the popular market were first created as paintings. We reproduce in color the third episode, *The Orgy* (Plate 129), from *A Rake's Progress.* The scene is largely self-explanatory, except for the portraits of Roman emperors (each but Nero's with its head cut out) and the staff and lantern by Tom's chair (probably trophies of some drunken prank). It is worth mentioning also that the woman spitting gin across the table at her rival is not an invention. Hogarth witnessed such an incident while visiting Moll King's Tavern with an artist friend, one Francis Hayman. Hogarth knew these brothel-taverns and their inmates well; if the bawds in the picture are not portraits they are close to it.

Toulouse-Lautrec's Paris

This brothel scene is chosen for illustration to make a comparison with Toulouse-Lautrec's *Salon in the Rue des Moulins* (Plate 130), painted in 1895. Hogarth's painting, whatever

Figure 22

its moral content in other ways, is unconcerned with his prostitutes except as accessories to the narrative of Tom's adventures. He tells us that loose company leads a foolish young man to ruin, but he does not indicate that the women are engaged in anything more distressing than a rollicking and profitable evening. In other words, the human condition is not involved in this illustration of a social evil except in the most roundabout way.

Now it is almost as heretical to suggest that the art of Toulouse-Lautrec has moral and compassionate social values as it is to say that Hogarth's is not dominated by them. But Toulouse-Lautrec's *Salon in the Rue des Moulins*, referring to a house frequented by the artist, is an intensely moral picture, in spite of its "immoral" theme, and subjective, in spite of its apparent reportorial objectivity. Each figure in the painting is a portrait of an inmate of this particular *maison close;* the seated one facing us (*Figure 22*) is the madame of the place. Instead of Hogarth's hilarious orgy we have here an expression of infinite lassitude, a suggestion of stagnant air where the spirit languishes, a mood with as little to do with hope as it does with hopelessness. Hogarth preaches that the wages of sin are madness and death; in Toulouse-Lautrec's world, they are infinite boredom. The central portrait (the profile, *Figure 22*) is an image of the desiccation of the human spirit. The other women are stultified into brutish semiconsciousness.

Hogarth's "moral comedies" take place in the fashionable half-world of the early eighteenth century; Toulouse-Lautrec's painting concentrates on Parisian bohemia at the end of the nineteenth. Both men are quite specific in their incidental references. (Toulouse-Lautrec's salon is already taking on the air of a period room, as Hogarth's interiors have long since done.) The difference we find in the painters, when we compare the brothel scene from *A Rake's Progress* with *Salon in the Rue des Moulins*, is that Hogarth is interested in people typed as social phenomena, and Toulouse-Lautrec is interested in people as individuals affected by the structure of society.

There comes a point where what we have been calling social consciousness merges with a more general consciousness of the human condition within the complexities of the world. Toulouse-Lautrec's *Salon in the Rue des Moulins* reaches this point; it would be hard to say whether it is more a comment on prostitution or more a comment on human beings who happen to be prostitutes. In that respect it stands midway between Hogarth's social observation and the comment on humanity in Ivan Albright's extraordinary painting, *Into the World There Came a Soul Named Ida* (Plate 131).

This mass of flesh, luminous with decay, pitted, scarred, and swollen with time, partially covered with bits of imitation silk—this piteous image may or may not be that of a prostitute, but it is certainly an image of the mortality of the flesh and of the spirit. By the clothes, dressing table, and knick-knacks, all of them shoddy machine products of the most painful ugliness and repellent vulgarity, this double mortality is linked to some evils of our civilization—its crassness and especially its exploitation of mediocrity. To that extent the picture is a social comment whether it was intended as one or not. The picture is not a tragic one since the subject is completely without nobility, a pathetic creature mercilessly painted. But the social implications are no less disturbing for being inherent in the subject rather than propounded by the artist.

With the exception of Botticelli's allegory, the paintings we have examined as social comment or social record have been on the whole realistic. Their realism has ranged from Shahn's near-caricature to David's neoclassical idealism, from Daumier's broad generalization of form to Albright's microscopic detail, from Trumbull's prosaic reconstruction to Rivera's decorative patterning. The use of realism is not surprising; fantasy by definition is useless to the artist as a social critic.

Figure 23

Blume's Rome

The artist as a fantast or visionary is the subject of our next portfolio, but we conclude this one with a painting so unusual that fantasy and sociopolitical content are inseparable, Peter Blume's *The Eternal City* (Plate 132).

The painting was completed in 1937 after several years of work following the artist's visit to Rome in 1932. It was the heyday of Mussolini's power as Il Duce. His fascist state was presenting every surface indication of Italian rejuvenation. Trains ran on time, as they had never done before in Italy. Tourists were always pointing this miracle out uncomfortably, finding this practical convenience more significant than the brutality and violence they read about in editorials but never met face to face (*Figure 23*). The full fascist potential had not yet been revealed by the events in Germany that were to make Mussolini's Italy only an amateurish preface to a full demonstration of man's capacity for evil.

Blume's picture shows Mussolini as a scareface leaping out of a jack-in-the-box. Weightless upon its paper stalk, the head was inspired by a papier-mâché statue of the dictator seen by the artist in Rome. With its brilliant green face and bright red lips it is a shocking dissonance (the painter's own word) in the color scheme. Blume writes, "It hurt me aesthetically to paint the head but . . . the question of harmony was superseded by other considerations."

What these other considerations are should

be apparent in the surrounding elaborate fantasy-allegory. Anyone who has visited Rome—and for that matter most people who have not—will recognize that *The Eternal City* is a composite of familiar elements like the underground corridors of the Colosseum, the pillared monuments of the Forum, the vaults of the catacombs, a shrine of the late baroque period, and the bell tower of an early medieval church. These references to the past do not insist on Rome's grandeur; corruption and decay are everywhere, culminating in a pile of broken sculpture and architectural fragments in the foreground, where a miserable beggar sits. Yet all of it is more substantial than the Halloween jack-in-the-box Duce springing from it. The luxuriant vines and the tree may be symbolical of the city's eternal vitality, its capacity for rebirth, just as the peaks in the background, which depict Italy's geographical entity, suggest also an eternity and indestructibility reducing the fascist regime to an affair of the moment.

The Eternal City was unfavorably received upon its first exhibition in this country but has advanced steadily in critical appreciation. It is one of those pictures that grow and change in meaning, seeming to have a life of their own independent of the artist's intention. If at first it could be interpreted as an allegory of centuries of decline and fall to the final degradation of domination by a pasteboard ogre, the allegory is now transformed into a prophecy of his fall. In the first case the title *The Eternal City* would be ironical; in the second, implicative. In either case the picture's ability to hold us and to offer different interpretations of its all-inclusive detail arises less from its political and historical allegory than its magical visionary nature. And in its character as a vision it serves as a point of departure for our next portfolio, the last in this series.

Notes on the Painters

Francisco de Goya, 1746-1828, Spanish

121. THE EXECUTIONS OF THE THIRD OF MAY, 1814–15

Oil on canvas. Height 8'8⅝". The Prado Museum, Madrid

Photo by Anderson

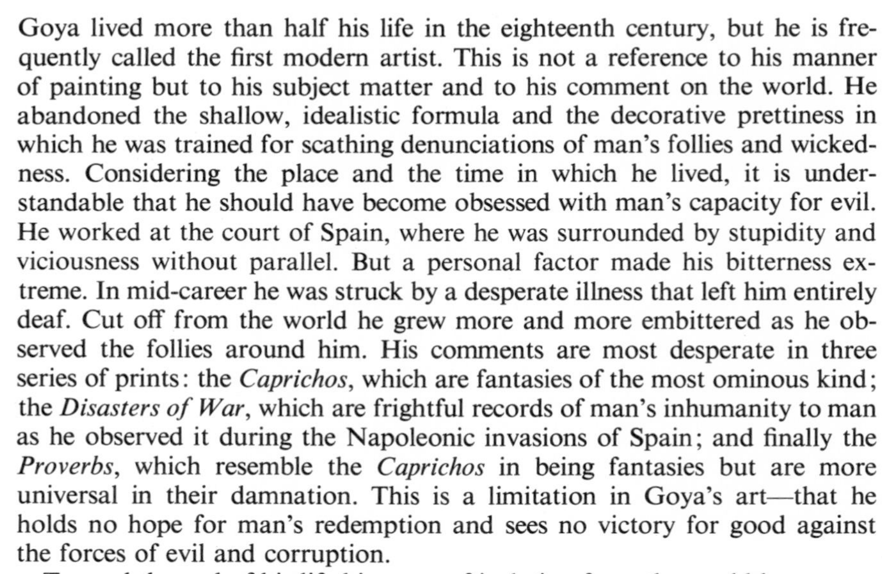

Goya lived more than half his life in the eighteenth century, but he is frequently called the first modern artist. This is not a reference to his manner of painting but to his subject matter and to his comment on the world. He abandoned the shallow, idealistic formula and the decorative prettiness in which he was trained for scathing denunciations of man's follies and wickedness. Considering the place and the time in which he lived, it is understandable that he should have become obsessed with man's capacity for evil. He worked at the court of Spain, where he was surrounded by stupidity and viciousness without parallel. But a personal factor made his bitterness extreme. In mid-career he was struck by a desperate illness that left him entirely deaf. Cut off from the world he grew more and more embittered as he observed the follies around him. His comments are most desperate in three series of prints: the *Caprichos*, which are fantasies of the most ominous kind; the *Disasters of War*, which are frightful records of man's inhumanity to man as he observed it during the Napoleonic invasions of Spain; and finally the *Proverbs*, which resemble the *Caprichos* in being fantasies but are more universal in their damnation. This is a limitation in Goya's art—that he holds no hope for man's redemption and sees no victory for good against the forces of evil and corruption.

Toward the end of his life his sense of isolation from the world became so extreme and his disgust with the men around him reached such a point that he retired to his villa outside Madrid, which came to be known as the Quinta del Sordo (Deaf Man's Villa). Here he painted some of the most nightmarish pictures in the history of art, visions of witches and congresses of monsters. At the very end of his life he exiled himself to France, finishing his life in Bordeaux, where to the last he continued to work with characteristic fierceness and vigor.

Sandro Botticelli, 1444/45-1510, Italian

122. CALUMNY, ABOUT 1494

Tempera on wood. Height 24⅜". The Uffizi Gallery, Florence

Botticelli as the master of linear delights has already been discussed in Portfolio 5 in connection with his *La Primavera.* The reader may be interested in comparing his use of line in *Calumny* with that of the earlier picture. In the allegory of trial and execution the line is more complex—knotted and tortured with intensity, in contrast to the lovely flowing and rippling character of the pagan allegory.

Ben Shahn, born 1898, American

123. THE PASSION OF SACCO AND VANZETTI, 1931–32

Tempera on canvas. Height 7′½″. The Whitney Museum of American Art, New York

Shahn is a Lithuanian-born painter who came to America as a child. *The Passion of Sacco and Vanzetti* is typical of the uncompromising directness of his early style, when he used bold, flat design, frequently harsh in color, to drive home his statement. More recently he has abandoned these very forceful statements for more obscure allegories in which fantasy plays a large part. His color, also, still flat and bright but subtler, is frequently bizarre, in harmony with the almost eerie character he can give such ordinary things as streets, vagabonds, and old buildings. The attraction of his new style from the point of view of decorativeness (its least important element) is such that a whole school of commercial art has risen from it, and his work is virtually plagiarized for everything from record album covers to fabrics.

John Trumbull, 1756-1843, American

124. THE DECLARATION OF INDEPENDENCE, 1786–94

Oil on canvas. Height 20″. Yale University Art Gallery, New Haven

Trumbull had better ideas on painting than he ever managed to carry out. The rather pedestrian character of *The Declaration of Independence* is typical of all Trumbull's completed work. It is distressing to find in his quick sketches a real feeling for dramatic painting that he apparently thought unworthy, or worthless, and managed all too successfully to weed out of his important work. The son of a governor of Connecticut, educated at Harvard, a student of painting in England and, by observation, in Paris, he tried to conform to the classical academic taste of the day without realizing that his talent lay in other directions. Trumbull was not very successful; he was sixty years old when, after many frustrations and disappointments, he received his commission for *The Declaration of Independence* and the other panels in the rotunda of the Capitol. He worked on them eight years, and although he lived to be eighty-seven these were his last—in fact, his only—important commissions.

Eugène Delacroix, 1798-1863, French

125. LIBERTY LEADING THE PEOPLE, 1830

Oil on canvas. Height 8′½″. The Louvre Museum, Paris

Delacroix, the great romantic painter, has been discussed in Portfolio 6. Here we might compare his career with Trumbull's. Trumbull sought to impose classical academic disciplines upon himself; Delacroix, living in France, the country where they were most rigid, revolted against them and managed not only to free himself but to free painting. That is, he established the right of the painter to paint as he pleased, in defiance of conventional painters if need be. It may be interesting to note that when Goya visited Paris as a very old man, he saw the work of Delacroix, then just at the beginning of his career, and approved. In his isolation in Spain Goya had made a similar revolution many years before, but unlike Delacroix he had not had to fight a powerful established group of academic painters in order to do so.

Jacques Louis David, 1748-1825, French

126. THE DEATH OF SOCRATES, 1787

Oil on canvas. Height 51". The Metropolitan Museum of Art, Wolfe Fund, 1931

David had a long career in which his painting and the political upheavals of his country were closely interrelated, a career unique in the history of artists. As a young man he was one of the group of talented students given an allowance (today we would call it a fellowship) by the king to study at the Royal Academy of Painting and Sculpture. He won its most coveted award, the Prix de Rome, which paid his expenses for a further period of study in Italy. Half by accident his *Death of Socrates* was adopted as a symbol of the Revolutionary party's ideal of self-sacrifice, and when the Revolution came David was carried with it into political power. He was an influential member of the governing body and was among the men who voted death for his former patron the king, who was guillotined. When dissensions arose within the party itself, David narrowly escaped execution and was imprisoned instead. In another sudden shift of authority he was released, and Napoleon, rising to power, made David his official painter. David had been an art dictator during the Revolution; he now became one under Napoleon. Finally, when Napoleon fell, David fled to Brussels where he finished his life in comfortable exile. No man has wielded a bigger stick in the history of art than David. He happened also to be a very fine painter, but he found no students who could live up to his demanding standards, which were so severe and restricting to individual expression that a revolt against them was inevitable, the revolt led by Delacroix.

François Boucher, 1703-1770, French

127. THE TOILET OF VENUS, 1751

Oil on canvas. Height 42⅝". The Metropolitan Museum of Art, bequest of William K. Vanderbilt, 1920

Boucher was court painter to Madame de Pompadour, the mistress of Louis XV. His fresh, artificial, sweetly tinted style with its air of feminine seductiveness permeated the décor of the period. Boucher designed tapestries, painted many portraits of La Pompadour, and filled fashionable boudoir panels with his pretty, pink nudes, who were perfectly at home in the deliciously artificial surroundings of the rococo style, then in its heyday. Boucher is not admired by many people today, but he is an extremely attractive painter once his artificiality is accepted. He is a great stylist and an impeccable technician.

Diego Rivera, 1886-1957, Mexican

128. THE LIBERATION OF THE PEON, 1931

Frescoed panel. Height 6'2". The Philadelphia Museum of Art

Rivera and his frescoes have already been discussed in Portfolio 8. As explained there many of his most important works are incorporated with the walls of buildings in Mexico. He felt strongly that "the new order of things" called for a new form of expression in art and that "the logical place for this art . . . belonging to the populace was on the walls of public buildings."

The Liberation of the Peon in Philadelphia is a slightly revised version of an outstanding fresco painted by Rivera for the Ministry of Education in Mexico City. The composition is somewhat tighter in this second treatment of the subject, and there has been some slight rearrangement of the figures. But both versions, as has often been remarked, are reminiscent of traditional representations of the Descent from the Cross.

William Hogarth, 1697-1764, British

129. THE RAKE'S PROGRESS: III, THE ORGY, ABOUT 1733

Oil on canvas. Height 24½". Sir John Soane's Museum, London

Hogarth, like several other artists considered in this portfolio, was something of a revolutionary against the established painters of his time. He railed against the successful portraitists as "face painters." His own conviction was that the face should be painted as a revelation of character and personality, not as a prettified mask having nothing to do with the sitter except to bear a flattering resemblance. As a result he had a hard time finding portrait commissions. To make ends meet he did several series of storytelling pictures and had them engraved to be published in large editions at moderate prices. These ventures were successful. People liked the prints for their jolly storytelling but frequently missed the depth of the social comments Hogarth was making.

Henri de Toulouse-Lautrec, 1864-1901, French

130. SALON IN THE RUE DES MOULINS, 1895

Oil on canvas. Height 43⅞". The Albi Museum, France

Toulouse-Lautrec has become almost too well known as a character in a successful film and many partially accurate biographies. This painter who could use his brush like a scalpel has been discussed in Portfolios 5 and 10.

Ivan Le Lorraine Albright, born 1897, American

131. INTO THE WORLD THERE CAME A SOUL NAMED IDA, 1927–30

Oil on canvas. Height 56¼". The Art Institute of Chicago

Albright was born in Chicago and works there now. It is enlightening, in view of the nature of his art, to know that in the First World War he did surgical drawings for a medical unit to which he was attached.

Peter Blume, born 1906, American

132. THE ETERNAL CITY, 1934–37

Oil on composition board. Height 34". The Museum of Modern Art, New York, Mrs. Simon Guggenheim Fund

Blume was born in Russia but was brought to America as a child and grew up in Brooklyn. Like Albright he is too individual a painter to fall easily into a general classification, but, also like Albright, his extremely detailed, precise representation and fantastic combinations of objects relate him to surrealism. Both men, however, extend beyond the personal eccentricities typical of surrealist painters to a field of wider comment.